Virtue

of

the

Gods

The First Letter to Aloysius

Kevin Michel

Virtue of the Gods: The First Letter to Aloysius

Note from the Author

This work is the first letter to my friend Aloysius regarding the "Virtue of the Gods." It has been made available to you the reader, so that you may also benefit. In the letter, I discuss the first virtue required to be one with the gods – a god walks through fire! The reader may be inspired to assume his/her true nature as a divine being. The reader may come to see the responsibility which he/she has to create a heaven on Earth, and throughout this universe.

Contents

Dear Aloysius,

I no longer have control over my writing, as I no longer seek such control. I have been afraid – afraid of what I might say if I wrote unencumbered. I have been afraid of what I might say if I did not spare a thought for the audience as I typed. I do a disservice to humanity if I continue to censor my work. I do a disservice to humanity if I allow fear to keep me from exploring ideas, and if I allow fear to stop me from saying that which may be better left unsaid. This is why I write to you Aloysius, and maybe you publish the work, and maybe you do not, but I know that as I write to you, I can express myself most freely, and I can share perspectives that may be most useful to yourself and to others. I know you can read this first letter Aloysius because your intellectual curiosity is at such a high level, and your openness to experience is clinically high. Yet, this is one of those letters that not everyone should read – this letter may be just for you, or for others like you. I wish you the best!

Introduction

Kevin Michel sends greetings to his friend Aloysius. What I write to you is in part a reminder and in part a warning. The message is that the various gods which so many people worship today are in fact not the masters of humanity, but are our peers. Even the gods themselves when represented in ancient texts have allegedly said this to humanity, yet few of us listen. In one such example, using the Christian god, Psalm 82:6, "I have said: 'You are gods; you are all sons of the Most High.'" With the Norsk, Roman, and Greek gods, the defining attribute of them are certain powers and certain virtues, and a significant longevity. Yet who can say that the human being is without great power and great longevity? Only those who enjoy weakness will say such. Many human beings are intent on clinging to that sort of weakness and victimhood, instead of embracing their true nature as powerful beings with great agency, and the potential for significant longevity, and significant influence on this planet and ultimately influence throughout the universe. In this letter I call on you to embrace your nature as a god, and to live with the virtue of the gods.

Maximum Virtue

For Aloysius, it is not acceptable that you should be weak. There is no eternal law, force, or deity that is forbidding you from achieving the extremes of greatness for all eternity. Yes, it may seem that your life is short compared to the apparent infinity of the universe, and yes, your life appears short when compared to the myths of Zeus, Apollo, or Kratos. The seeming shortness of your life is an illusion, for certainly your life can be as long as you choose it to be, and even longer still. Shall your life cease tomorrow, or shall it end one million years hence, the reality from your perspective is that your life endured for all of time. Your terminal breath shall be a long breath out, and the time between that last exhale and the next inhale, shall be the balance of eternity. In the intervening moment between those breaths you shall not have awareness of an infinity of occurrences throughout the universe, but that is only a miniscule difference between that infinity of none awareness which you have right now.

Aloysius, it shall serve you well to develop the aptitude for deep breathing, and focused awareness in your daily life. Now inhale through the nose, and then hold it for five seconds, and then exhale for seven seconds through the mouth; then inhale for five, then exhale for seven, and then in again, then, after the next exhale, you wait for the passage of all remaining time and existence. Even as your body decays, the next breath in, shall be pending – those are the breaths of an eternal being.

As a human, you do not ask for permission to inhale, and you request no guarantee of life, neither life eternal nor even life in the next moment. For you are life, and life persists for as long as you persist – yet nothing is promised. The threat of death carries no weight for someone who has no need for the breath nor need for any specific pleasant accommodation.

"Whoever tries to save his life will lose it, but whoever loses his life will preserve it."

– Luke 17:34

Aloysius, I quote that line not because it is the truth, for no faith has a monopoly on truth, and it is well known that not one of the many great books was written by a god – all by their own admission, have been the works of man. I focus on the Christian book since it is the most prevalent in your culture, that book having been written by man and as with all such books, alleged to have been inspired by god. Mind you, the very same man wrote that book who, if we follow the logic, is capable of "bearing false witness against [his] neighbor." Why would an all powerful god ask you Aloysius to trust the words of your fellow dishonest man, and then to have you punished for all eternity if you fail to be so gullible? The Christian god knows that man is dishonest, thus the commandment forbidding the "bearing of false witness." If god thought man to be honest then that commandment would have been unnecessary. An all powerful god would never entrust the fate of your soul to the words of dishonest human beings. I can assure you that an all powerful god would speak to you directly on matters that relate to the fate of your soul. A human being who is seeking to control and deceive you would say to you *do not question the book, for it is holy,* and to *trust in faith.* An all powerful god would **not** establish blind faith to be a virtue, for blind faith is a virtue only of fools. Blind faith is not a virtue of the gods. Foolishness is not a virtue of the gods. I understand that so many of us, as children, were told that faith is a virtue, but faith is no virtue. Faith is lazy. Faith is an unwillingness to engage in investigation and reason.

Faith is for the blind and a powerful god would want you to clearly see the truth, without ambiguity, so that you may choose the right path.

"When I was a child, I spoke as a child, I understood as a child, I thought as a child: but when I became a man, I put away childish things."

– 1 Corinthians 13:11

Aloysius you know that man has lied to you, because no god would say to you that you must bow down and worship. You are not asked to be subservient, and if any god asks you to be subservient, and to worship him/her, then that is not a powerful god, for powerful gods need nothing added to them. Mighty gods do not crave your worship, your admiration, or your flattery. Those are not desires of gods, those are desires of men.

The gods do not listen to prayers, for their reasoning is countless steps in advance of our own, and essentially every event to unfold has been considered or even adjudicated through their own will. However the gods do not propose that the future is fixed, and they expect of us that we act responsibly and take the action we can to determine our own fate. If you seek to pray, the gods respect it most when your prayers take the form of measurable goals, actions, and sustained processes. From the perspective of the gods, to say "thoughts and prayers" as a response to situations within our control, is both a sin and a taunt. Spare your thoughts and prayers, and get to work.

What can be said of the gods, can also be said of man, that is, the gods admire in man the virtues that are in their own image. Exempli gratia, the gods admire strength, the gods admire courage, and the gods admire wisdom – to state this differently, the gods admire the virtues that are godlike. Aloysius, you are called to get off of your knees, and to embody the virtue of the gods, and to be your true nature, which is the nature of the gods. In this first of seven letters, I share with you the virtues of the gods that you would do well to emulate if you are to be one who can stand in the company of the gods, and if you are to live a life of significance whilst in this universe. No doubt the first virtue is the willingness to think, and to question, and to engage in reasoning and logistical processes.

Having the virtue of the gods and being able to stand confidently in the presence of the gods is not about pleasing your ego – having the virtue of the gods and being able to stand with them is about making a better world, and making a difference. It is ultimately about feeding the hungry, healing the sick, and building up the capabilities of the poor. That Aloysius, if you are to be truly virtuous, is what you must do – feed the hungry, heal the sick, and strengthen, house, and clothe the poor. Is that not what has been said were the actions of the Christian god in his time on earth? For I promise you, much of the truth has been lost in translation, and much of the original documentation was falsified, and warped by man's own malevolence, and twisted to serve man's own ego and predilections, and crafted by groupings of men seeking control over the squalid masses – and if the other gods were to put you up for trial, I can declare to you that the questions asked will **not** be:

"Did you wear the correct hat?"

"Did you mix linen and wool?"

"What specific religion did you follow? Was it the right religion? Did you decipher the nature of the real prophet?"

"Did you eat an unclean meat?"

"Did you do things at the moment when the Earth

was at a certain point in the celestial orbit?"

Those are not the questions! I assure you, that is not the test. You shall be queried regarding your contributions to the quality of life of your fellow man, helping, feeding, clothing, healing, you know, godlike stuff, not trivial, benign, or banal things. There are questions about care and concern for your fellow man. There are no questions about penises and how to use them and where they should go – those are childish and silly things, suitable for petty and small minds. I know Aloysius that you do not see the gods as being so petty that they would spend their time talking about rituals, and specific days, and what meats were eaten and when. Those are not the concerns of mighty gods, those are blatantly and manifestly the concerns of the weakest and most manipulative of men.

A God Walks Through Fire

The gods face challenges, and the gods impose challenges. The challenges created by gods often appear as infinite challenges, but they are never infinite. A seemingly infinite challenge can be overcome with applied wisdom over time. I have heard one sick account which seems ripe for inspiring fear in children and in adults with childish minds, the story goes that one of the gods has prepared fiery coffins to meet you in the next world. The coffins are made of pure flame, and the lids are of an unearthly weight. You, now in the afterworld, but with a body that is apparently human, struggles and writhes in pain. There is weeping and gnashing of teeth, and bellows from the burns. What a sadistic god! Torturing those who are weak or who have by some measure failed is *not* a virtue of a god, so this is either not a powerful god, or more likely the stories are false, or this is a temporary trial that the god presents.

Aloysius, I know many a boy who could be set on the right path if the right intervention is done at the right time, and even some adults can be reformed given sufficient resources. for example, this is why some countries like Norway have lower recidivism rates for prisoners, with offenders committing serious crimes once and then never again; whereas in the U.S. the offenders commit repeatedly. The difference being the way the convicts are treated by the system, and the efforts toward rehabilitation with punishment, so we know that serious offenders can be reformed by human policies, yet people allege that the Christian god's solution is eternal fire, and eternal punishment for finite crimes? Ye of little faith! An all powerful god can reform all manner of men.

So in this story, there you are in your fiery coffin, and you scream in pain all of day one, you scream in pain all of day two, you scream in pain all of day three, and then what? Do you scream in pain all of day four, day five, day six? Or do you take a moment of reflection to ponder the nature of your pain? What do we know about pain in the human body? Pain in the body is information. There are receptors in human tissue called nociceptors, and those send signals to the processing centers in the brain whenever the nociceptors detect that there is ongoing tissue damage, or the potential for tissue damage. The brain converts those signals to a form of pressing anxiety and to a form of aversive motivation. That is all pain is – pain is subjective information. That is one of the reasons persons can experience phantom pains in limbs that have been amputated and no longer exist. Consider, in your coffin furnace, are your tissues being damaged by the combustion? Certainly not, otherwise the process would not last very long. Is there potential then for tissue damage? Again, no, for there is clearly no realistic potential for damage if such damage then never occurs. So what is your pain then? What are you screaming about?

The human body has the ability to produce pain, and the human body has the ability to suppress, and completely ignore pain. On day seven, you come to terms with this. On day seven, you realize that sensation is not reality. You realize that your mind is what retains control of the world around you. It is the mind that creates happiness, joy, or suffering. The mind that maketh you weak, and the mind that maketh you strong. You realize, that you must possess the virtue of the gods in order to stand with them.

Did you know that in your Earthly body, one of the neurotransmitters that the brain uses to suppress pain is the neurotransmitter called serotonin? Low serotonin levels, such as that which occurs in persons who fall into clinical depression, lead to a reduced ability to suppress pain. High serotonin, means easier suppression of pain. Your serotonin level is determined largely by how you view your standing in the social hierarchy in which you find yourself. If you see yourself as being at the top of the social hierarchy, then your serotonin spikes, and if you see yourself at the bottom it quickly falls. When you see yourself as a god, you increase your perceived status, you embrace your infinite ability to create your own mental state, and fire ceases to be relevant. You stop feeling the pain of the fire, and you begin to feel the joy of the fire. Promptly, the infinity of signals being sent by your nociceptors shall cease, and now with the channels clear your brain can send signals to the spiritual equivalent of the pectoral muscles, and you realize, the lid on your coffin was not that heavy after all. You stop weeping, you enjoy the pain, you get on with what needs to be done.

You have been baptized by fire and passed the test, and the gods now respect your virtue. The god of fire then casually says to you that you could have taken that step a lot sooner. You did not need to seemingly die in order to get to this breakthrough. You could have realized it when you were still on Earth. Raise your status, be a god, do what must be done with virtue, to create a heaven on Earth. The first virtue of the gods is to walk through your fire now, and to enjoy the pain. Aloysius, you must walk through fire now. Walking through fire is a focus on the process as you pursue worthy goals. Walking through fire means every time your attention is pulled away from your focus, that you are able to bring your attention right back to that which is most important for your long term progress to those worthy goals. This is why you concentrate on the breath in mindfulness meditation. 5 seconds inhale, 7 seconds exhale, always with attention on the breath. It is a practice that when done consistently, shall strengthen your fortitude and mental muscle. That focus is what you must do until what you believe will be your last breath. Yet it shall not be your last breath, for you are truly eternal, for with focus and virtue, you are one with the gods.

Conclusion

I must return to other affairs Aloysius, yet I shall write you again soon with more exploration of this issue. I wish you confidence, and focus, as you walk through your fire – for you create your own fire Aloysius; you judge yourself. You are the god of fire! Are you sadistic or merciful? Are you able to help, and lift up, and help reform you fellow man, or do you just cast him away, label him hopeless, and burn him? For verily, I say onto you, as ye judge your fellow man, so shall you be judged. Aloysius, I wish you the virtues of the gods. We shall correspond again soon, until then, farewell.

Made in the USA
Monee, IL
07 July 2026